Mel Bay's Modern
GUITAR METHOD GRADE 1

by William Bay

Modern Guitar Method Grade 1, Guitar Studies is a carefully graded series of exercises, solos, duets, and chord studies which ideally supplements **Mel Bay's** *Modern Guitar Method, Grade 1* and the note reading section of **Mel Bay's** *Guitar Class Method.* This text, in addition, will be a valuable aid to any beginning guitar student and the content will augment and enhance learning regardless of the basic instructional text being used.

1 2 3 4 5 6 7 8 9 0

Visit us on the Web at www.melbay.com — E-mail us at email@melbay.com

Marching

Out West

Outer Space

Inner Space

Finger Builder

3

2nd String Studies

B-C-D

B-D-B

Song

Children's Song

Waterfall

Re-Count!

For thorough study into daily practice and technique building, see *Mel Bay's Guitar Handbook* book and companion stereo play-along cassette.

1-2-3

$\frac{3}{4}$ Song

Floating

1-2-Rest

Dotted Half

Back to $\frac{4}{4}$

B-D-D

Last Resort

5

Studies on the 1st & 2nd Strings

Surprise Song

Indian Drum

E-B-Song

Turkey Waltz

C-B-C

6

Finger Builder

Waltz of the Hippos

March

Flower Song

Western Song

Studies on the 3rd String

G-A

Count

Count Again

All Smiles

Au Clair De La Lune

Jingle Bells

Studies on the 1st, 2nd, & 3rd Strings

Yankee Doodle

Bile Dem Cabbage

Jacob's Ladder

Space Walk

Old Smokey

Boogie

Down in the Valley

Climbing the Strings

Staircase

Studies on the 4th String

D-E-F

Eighth Notes

Mystery

Hole In My Bucket

Indian Song

Minor Melody

Count

11

Studies on the 1st, 2nd, 3rd,& 4th Strings

D Minor

Bucking Bronco

Sourwood Mountain

Finger Builder

Chord Song

For thorough study into daily practice and technique building, see *Mel Bay's Guitar Handbook* book and companion stereo play-along cassette.

Studies on the 5th String

5th String Song

Walking

Running

Waltz

Skipping

"A" Dance

A-C-B

Bugle Call

Studies on the 1st, 2nd, 3rd, 4th, & 5th Strings

Low A

Chinese Checkers

Frankie & Johnny

Hometown Waltz

Polka

The Riddle Song

Sweet Betsy from Pike

Blow the Man Down

C Scale Study

The Clock
(Duet)

The Yellow Rose of Texas

Teacher Accomp.

Marching Song

Teacher Accomp.

Studies on the 6th String

Big E

Elephant Waltz

Re-Count!

Teacher Accomp.
Goin' Down the Road Feelin' Bad

Teacher Accomp.
Little Brown Jug

Cape Cod Girls

Crawdad Song

We Wish You a Merry Christmas

High "A" Studies

Singing Canary

Left Footed Waltz

Blow Ye Winds

Running the Notes

19

Chord Studies

For thorough study into daily practice and technique building, see *Mel Bay's Guitar Handbook* book and companion stereo play-along cassette.

My Country Tis of Thee

Green Grow the Lilacs

Chord Song

The "F" Chord

(Student plays the top 4 strings)

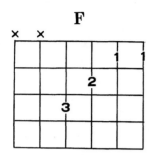

To play the F chord - make sure your left hand thumb is on the center of the back of the neck. If you wrap your thumb around the neck so that it touches the 6th string, you will have problems fingering the F chord.

Building the F chord

Play the following exercise until the tone sounds clear. You will start on the 1st fret and end on the 7th fret.

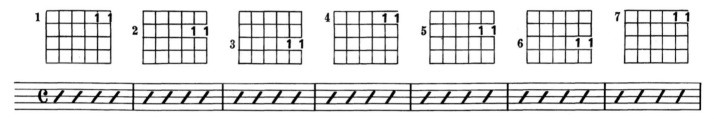

Now play this exercise from the 1st to the 7th fret until it sounds clear.

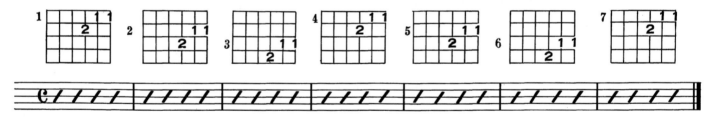

Play from 1st to 7th fret until it sounds clear.

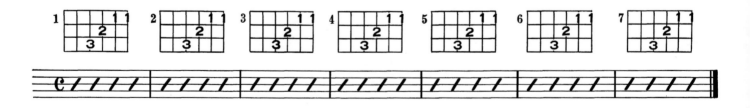

Faith of Our Fathers

Handel's Piece

Dance

23

Bass Solos With Chord Accompaniment

Oh, How I Love Jesus

Western Song

I'm On My Way

24

Oh Bury Me Not on the Lone Prairie

Teacher Accomp.

Red River Valley

Teacher Accomp.

Country Waltz

Teacher Accomp.

C Scale Studies

Chords in the Key of C Major

The key of C has three principal chords. They are C, F, and G7.

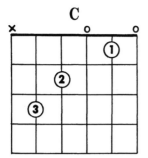

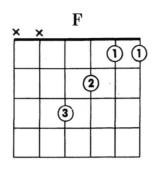

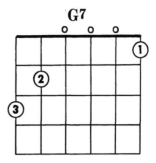

The circles indicate the positions to place your fingers.

Numerals inside circles indicate the fingers.

(×) over the strings means that the strings are not to be played.

(o) over the strings indicates the strings to be played open.

Place fingers on positions indicated by the circles and strike them all together.

Chord Studies in key of C

╱ = Strum chord Down Across strings

⊓ = Down - Up strum
↓ ↑

Down - Up

27

Wildwood Flower

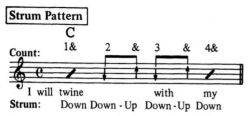

Strum down on beat 1. Strum down-up on beats 2 and 3. Strum down on beat 4.

1. I will twine with my ming - les of ra - ven black hair___

___ With the ro - ses so red and the li - lies so

fair.___ The myr - tle so bright with its

em - er - ald dew___ And the pale and the

lead - er and eyes look so blue.___

Standing in the Need of Prayer

2. Ain't my father or my mother, but it's me, oh, Lord.
3. Ain't the preacher or the deacon, but it's me, oh, Lord.
4. Ain't my neighbor or a stranger, but it's me, oh, Lord.

The Marine's Hymn

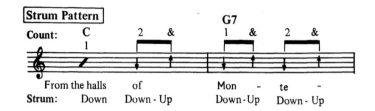

The Chords in the Key of A Minor

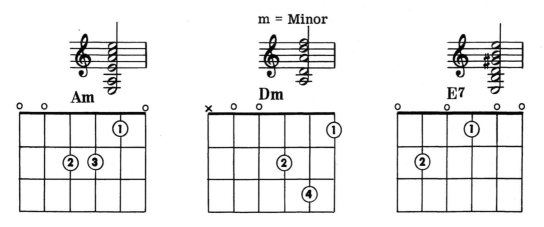

m = Minor

The key of Aminor has three principal chords. They are Am, Dm, and E7.

Chord Studies in the key of Am

✓ = Strum chord Down Across the Strings

↓ ↑ = Down – Up strum

Down - Up

For thorough study into daily practice and technique building, see *Mel Bay's Guitar Handbook* book and companion stereo play-along cassette.

Joshua "Fit" the Battle of Jericho
(Student Strums Chords-Teacher Plays Melody)

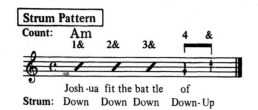

Patapan

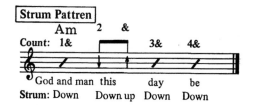

French Carol

The Master's Favorite

Guitar Duet

MAZAS, Op . 85
Arr. by Mel Bay

Duets

O For A Thousand Tongues

Hymn

Tallis Canon

A Minor Studies

Study Number 1

Study Number 2

Duet 'Ala' Bach

William Bay

37

G Scale Studies

Chords in the Key of G

G

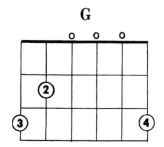

C

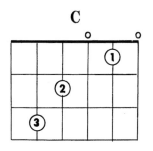

D7

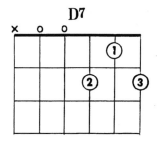

The key G has three principal chords: They are G, C, and D7.

Chord Studies in The key of G

╱ = Strum chord Down Across The Strings

↓ ↑ = Down - Up Strum

Down - Up

Blow, Ye Winds

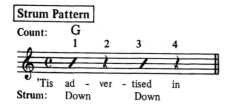

'Tis ad-ver-tised in Bos - ton, New York and Buf-fa - lo, Five

hun - dred brave A - mer - i - cans, A sail - ing for to go,___ sing - ing

blow ye winds in the morn - ing, And blow ye winds high ho!

Clear a-way your run-ning gear and blow, ye winds, high ho!

The Wabash Cannonball

From the great At - lan - tic O - cean to the wide Pa - cif - ic

shore, From the queen of flow - ing riv - ers to the south - land by the

shore, She's might y ___ tall and hand - some and quite well known by

all. How we love the "Choo Choo" of the Wa - bash Can - non - ball!

Go Tell It on the Mountain

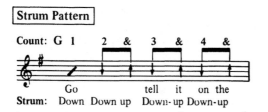

For thorough study into daily practice and technique building, see *Mel Bay's Guitar Handbook* book and companion stereo play-along cassette.

German Hymn
(Duet)

Arr. Bill Bay

means to hold
the note

Daydreaming
(Duet)

Bill Bay

The Chords in the Key of E Minor

The Chords in the key of E Minor are:

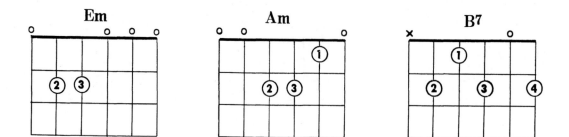

The key of E minor has three principal chords. They are Em, Am, and B7.

Chord Studies in the key of E minor

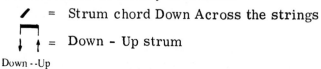

= Strum chord Down Across the strings

= Down - Up strum

Down --Up

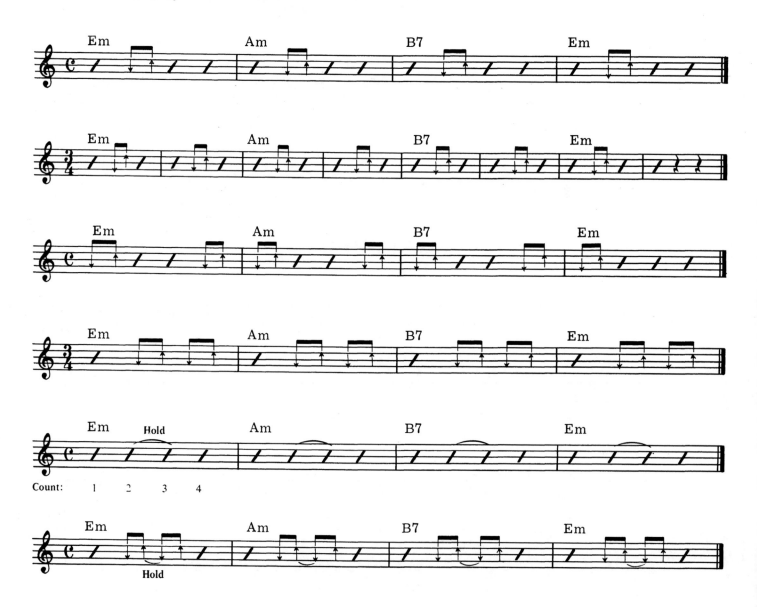

Count: 1   2   3   4

44

Wade In The Water

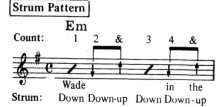

Spiritual

Chorus
1. Wade in the wa - ter, Wade in the wa-ter, chil - dren

Wade in the wa - ter, God's gon-na trou-ble these wa - ters.

See that band all__ dressed in white God's gon-na trou-ble these wa - ters,

looks like a band of the Is-ra-el - ites, God's gon-na trou-ble these wa - ters.

The D Chord

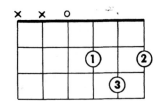

What Child Is This

E Minor Studies

Meditation
(Duet)

Bill Bay

Student plays top line only

Solos

Winds Through the Olive Trees

Hymn

Musetta's Waltz
From "La Boheme"

Puccini

Moderate, flowing tempo

rit.

Chorale

Bill Bay

Moderately